Amazing Animal Skills

MOVERS AND MAKERS

HOW ANIMALS BUILD AND USE TOOLS TO SURVIVE

ROBIN KOONTZ

mc **Marshall Cavendish**
Benchmark
New York

Special thanks to Donald E. Moore III, associate director of animal care at the Smithsonian Institution's National Zoo, for his expert reading of this manuscript.

Other Marshall Cavendish Offices: Marshall Cavendish International (Asia) Private Limited, 1 New Industrial Road, Singapore 536196 • Marshall Cavendish International (Thailand) Co Ltd. 253 Asoke, 12th Flr, Sukhumvit 21 Road, Klongtoey Nua, Wattana, Bangkok 10110, Thailand • Marshall Cavendish (Malaysia) Sdn Bhd, Times Subang, Lot 46, Subang Hi-Tech Industrial Park, Batu Tiga, 40000 Shah Alam, Selangor Darul Ehsan, Malaysia

Marshall Cavendish is a trademark of Times Publishing Limited

All websites were available and accurate when this book was sent to press.

Library of Congress Cataloging-in-Publication Data
Koontz, Robin Michal.
Movers and makers : how animals build and use tools to survive / Robin Koontz.
p. cm. — (Amazing animal skills)
Includes bibliographical references and index.
ISBN 978-0-7614-4910-2 (Print); 978-1-60870-603-7 (eBook)
1. Tool use in animals—Juvenile literature.2.
Animals—Habitations—Juvenile literature. I. Title. II. Series.
QL785.K658 2012
591.56'4—dc22
2010039660

EDITOR: Joy Bean   PUBLISHER: Michelle Bisson
ART DIRECTOR: Anahid Hamparian   SERIES DESIGNER: Kristen Branch

Photo research by Joan Meisel
Cover photo: Alain Mafart-Renodier/Photolibrary
The photographs in this book are used by permission and through the courtesy of: *Alamy*: Peter Arnold, 4; Kjell Sandved, 5; First Light, 1, 3, 7; Scott Camazine, 10; WorldFoto, 13; William Leaman, 15; Charles Stirling (Travel), 19; Premaphotos, 25(b); Arco Images GmbH, 26; infocusphotos.com, 31; Frans Lanting Studio, 33; Robert E Barber, 36; Dave Watts, 37; Michael Patrick O'Neill, 39; *Getty*: Jason Edwards, 7; Peter Litja, 14; Jeff Foott, 44; *Minden Pictures*: Norbert Wu, 9; Tui De Roy, 24; *Photo Researchers Inc.*: Michel & Christine Denis-Huot, 17; *Photolibrary*: Oxford Scientific (OSF), 23, 28, 30, 41; Age fotostock, 43; *SuperStock*: IndexStock, 25(t).

Printed in Malaysia [T]
1 3 5 6 4 2

CONTENTS

CHAPTER ONE

HOMEMADE HAVENS

The animal world is filled with masterminds that use amazing and unusual skills to create a safe haven or catch a meal. Animals can spit, spin, glue, weave, weld, burrow, borrow, and form structures that protect or house from one to millions of creatures. Some animals can make use of special body parts or **excretions** to snag a snack. Others create clever tricks and traps to catch prey or lure a mate. Others make use of things like sticks, rocks, trash, or even their own bodies to build

A paper nautilus with her homemade shell.

4

a protective space or to catch a bite of dinner.

Some animals use spit and other **secretions** to construct a place to live. A type of octopus called a paper nautilus can make her own shell. The female secretes goo from her legs that forms into a thin shell around part of her body. She uses the shell as protection and as a place for her eggs to develop.

The peacock worm lives in shallow waters along the coasts of western Europe and in the Mediterranean. This sea creature also makes its own shell-like structure using body fluids. It spits out mucus and uses it to glue sand and mud into a tube that sticks up from the seafloor. The worm can hide inside and extend its feathery tentacles out the top to catch passing tiny creatures.

Beautiful Treasure

The remains of a delicate egg case made by a female paper nautilus are a rare find for a beachcomber. This animal's remains are hard to find, even though great numbers of them live in areas of the world such as Australia.

Peacock worms look like delicate flowers in the sea.

The worm scoots back inside its tube if something scary swims too close.

A caddis fly larva creates a homemade shell from spewed glue mixed with sand, shells, pebbles, and even garbage bits. It can duck inside the shell if a hungry fish swims nearby. A caddis fly larva will soon grow too large for its shell. That is no problem; it just builds another one. Eventually, it emerges as an adult caddis fly.

BODY BUILDERS

The water-holding frog of northern Australia uses its own skin as a hideaway. During the short rainy season, it gathers as much water as it can. Then the frog burrows deep into the mud, as deep as 3 feet (1 meter). It sheds its skin in one whole piece. Then the frog uses the skin as a cocoon-like sleeping bag while it waits for the next rain to come. It can wait for two years or more!

A HOUSE OF WAX

Honeybees are master spit homebuilders. They form honeycombs out of wax, which they produce from special glands. The bees can form thousands of perfect rows of six-sided cells. Each cell is used to either store food or give safe haven to developing young.

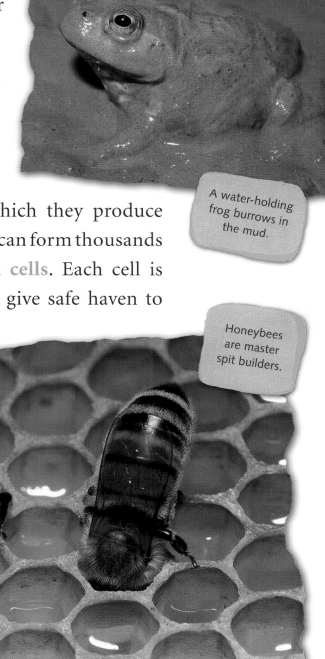

A water-holding frog burrows in the mud.

Honeybees are master spit builders.

CHAPTER TWO
CLEVER HUNTERS

Many animals use their spit or bodies for some unusual hunting strategies. The black heron lives around wetlands and lagoons in parts of Africa. When it's time to find some small fish to eat, this bird stands in the water and spreads its wings. Holding its wings out in front with its head tucked down, the heron forms a shady

A black heron creates a shady spot for tasty fish to hang out.

An anglerfish fishes for fish.

umbrella over the water. Small fish like shade. Shade gives them a safe place to hide from predators, such as birds that want to eat them. Meanwhile, the black heron can see them easily without the glare of the sun, so the heron can scoop up a meal of fish. Whoops!

The anglerfish has a built-in fishing pole that sticks out of its bumpy head. The pole is really a spine that has a fishlike lure dangling from the end. The anglerfish crawls around on the ocean floor, using its fins like feet and hands. It can wiggle its lure to attract a hungry fish. Once the

Fast Fact

An anglerfish can suck in a small fish so quickly that nearby fish don't even notice. An anglerfish can sit and eat from the same fish school for hours.

Fast Fact

The alligator
snapping turtle
is the largest
freshwater turtle
in North America.
It is listed as
a threatened
species. It can live
to be 100 years
old. A male can
weigh more than
200 pounds (90
kilograms).

fish gets close, the anglerfish sucks it in with its huge mouth, much like a vacuum cleaner.

The huge alligator snapping turtle lives in freshwater rivers, lakes, and ponds in the southeastern United States. It is a master at fishing without a pole. This turtle has a red growth in its mouth that looks a lot like a tasty, wiggly worm. The turtle sits still with its mouth open, waiting like a patient fisher. Soon a fish nibbles at the worm until—oops!—the fish finds out how this turtle got its snappy name.

Worms look yummy to many other animals, including lizards, mice, frogs, and birds. The death adder is a snake from Australia that has a clever adaptation for catching dinner. The end of its tail looks a lot like a tasty yellow-segmented worm. The poisonous snake camouflages itself in the surrounding sand so nothing

An alligator snapping turtle shows off its fishing lure.

10

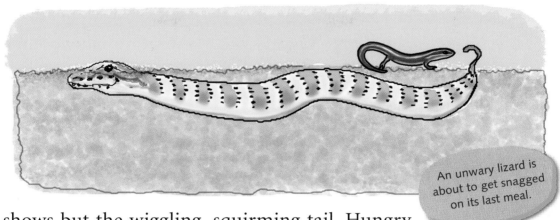

shows but the wiggling, squirming tail. Hungry animals come to take a bite of the "worm" and get eaten instead.

EIGHT-LEGGED TRAPPERS

Sometimes a house can serve as a handy trap for catching a meal. The trapdoor spider builds a tubelike tunnel in the ground where insects might walk. The opening of the tunnel has a trapdoor made of spider spit, silk, and dirt. The door has silk hinges to make it easy to open and close. The spider lives in the tunnel and uses it to protect its young. But trapping a meal is the main use for the tunnel. The spider will hold the trapdoor

A trapdoor spider invites a guest for dinner.

shut and wait for a vibration above that sounds like something tasty walking along. Snatch! The spider will throw open the door, grab the prey, and head back inside, shutting the door behind it.

A bolas spider can also trap its dinner. One type of bolas spider looks like a bird dropping and smells like a moth. This critter uses a single strand of silk to fish for moths. It spits a sticky glob on the end of the thread and swings it with a front leg. The glob sticks to a moth that was attracted

Fast Fact

The bolas spider is named after its hunting method. A real bolas is a rope with weights on the ends. It is thrown at a small animal or bird and gets tangled around its legs. Bolas were used as weapons for hunting by tribes in South America. Cattle ranchers, called gauchos, still use a kind of bolas today to catch small animals.

by the moth smell. The spider can swing the lure with great accuracy.

BUBBLE TRAP

Bubbles can make a good trap for getting food, too. The humpback whale blows bubbles from its blowhole to help round up a school of tasty fish. The whale circles below the surface of the ocean, blowing bubbles, forming a huge bubble net. Meanwhile, other humpback whales on the surface scream and wave flippers to help herd fish into the net of bubbles. Once the fish are corralled inside the bubble fence, the whales dive into the corral with mouths open. The team effort pays off in a big fish feast.

Humpback whales creating a nest of bubbles.

CHAPTER THREE

HANDY TOOLS

Many animals make smart use of available materials to help them enjoy a meal or build a home. One type of tiny, tree-dwelling ant makes use of a particular plant that grows in the Amazon rainforest. Several ants make a mix of

Fast Fact

Many ants have a special relationship with plants. The plant provides them with a place to live and catch food. In return, the ants help to keep pests from eating the plant.

plant fibers, fungus, and spit and spread it on the stem of their host plant. The goo creates a hard surface with holes all over it. The ants hide in the holes with their **mandibles** open. They try to snatch anything that walks along their trap. If the prey is too big for one ant to nab, several ants grab at the legs, stretch the creature, and sting it to death. Then they bite it into pieces and haul off the bits to their hungry colony.

Acorn woodpeckers also work together to store food for the family. Like most woodpeckers, they will drill a hole in a live or dead tree using their sharp beaks to create a nesting cavity. These birds also drill into branches and trees to store food, especially acorns. One family group will spend hours and hours creating little holes and

An acorn woodpecker stores acorns in its homemade pantry.

15

poking in acorns by the thousands. One storage tree might have as many as 50,000 stashed acorns.

Another bird makes use of tools for storing food. A shrike is a crow-size bird that eats mammals and other small birds as well as insects. Sometimes it kills more food that it can eat or feed to its babies. When that happens, the shrike will impale the extra food on the thorns of plants or barbed-wire fencing for safe keeping.

SMART CRACKER

Some food is not that easy to get to, such as food with a hard shell. Many animals have figured out how to crack open hard shells without a nutcracker. The otter lives in the Pacific Ocean. Its favorite foods, crabs and clams, are covered with shells. All the good meat is on the inside. The otter has figured out how to use a

An otter smacks a shell against his belly rock.

rock as a hammer. An otter will grab a rock from the seafloor and use it to pry out the critters that hide among the rocks. Then it will take the rock and its prize to the water's surface. The otter floats on its back in the seaweed with the rock resting on its belly. Crack! It slams the shellfish down on the belly rock and breaks it open. Dinnertime!

BIRD BRAINS

Birds also know a thing or two about using rocks. An Egyptian vulture drops stones on ostrich eggs until one cracks open. A bearded vulture breaks the brittle bones of dead animals by dropping them on rocky places. Then it can munch on the nutritious bone marrow inside. The golden eagle has figured out that the best way to get to a turtle is

An Egyptian vulture gets help from a rock to crack an egg.

through its shell. This eagle will grab a turtle in its claws and carry it high in the sky, then let the turtle plummet to the rocks below. If the first try doesn't do the trick, it will snatch up the turtle and drop it again. Look out below!

A crow that lives in New Caledonia, Australia, uses the "drop it on a rock" method to crack open snails. But it does much more than that to find other things to eat. It makes and uses tools. The New Caledonian crow is not the only bird to use tools. For instance, the woodpecker finch will hold a twig or cactus spine in its beak and use it to poke around in tree bark for insects. But the New Caledonian crow does more than that. It turns sticks and leaves into tools for grabbing food that is out of reach. The clever crow makes hooks from sticks by whittling

Feathered Toolmaker

Scientists have learned a lot about New Caledonian crows and other clever animals by studying them in captivity. Betty was one famous crow. Betty picked up a straight piece of wire, stuck it in a crack in a table, and bent it with her beak. She used her hook to snag food that had been placed out of her reach.

with its beak. It cuts leaves so they have a pointed shape and barbs. The crow holds this tool in its beak and uses it to pull out grubs and insects from logs and trees.

New Caledonian crows whittle sticks to poke around in small spaces.

NOSE GUARDS

Some animals rely on their noses to seek out and unearth tasty meals. The female bottlenose dolphin of western Australia has a beak of sorts that is called a **rostrum**. It digs deep in the ocean floor with its rostrum, looking for bottom-dwelling creatures like fish and crabs. But the rostrum is not hard like a bird's beak and can get stung by stinging fish or cut by sharp coral. This smart girl sticks her rostrum into a soft sea

Bottlenose dolphins have a nose for finding food.

sponge that cushions and protects the rostrum while she pokes around.

CAPTIVE AUDIENCE

Zookeepers, trainers, and others who deal with captive animals get to see how the animals perform some clever tricks. At the San Diego Zoo's Wild Animal Park, condors will follow keepers as they walk by. The big birds will poke at the keepers through the cage with sticks or feathers they hold in their beaks. Maybe they're saying, "Hey, it's time to feed us!"

MASTER TOOL USERS

Apes and monkeys are well-known tool users. Most of them have been studied in captivity, but many discoveries have also been made in the wild. The chimpanzee uses a stick to poke around in termite mounds. The termites crawl onto the stick and attack it. The clever chimp draws out the termite lollipop and licks it clean. The chimp has also been seen pounding on the tasty, spongy material in the crown of a palm tree. It spreads the tree's fronds apart to expose the crown. Then it breaks off a stiff frond and uses it to pound on the crown.

The pounding softens the material so it's easier to munch.

The chimpanzee likes nuts of all kinds. It will use a flat stone or a tree root as a base and bang down with another rock or club to split open nuts. A chimp will even use a stick as a spear. The chimp will gnaw on the end of a stick to make a sharp point. Then it will force the stick into a tree hole where it thinks a small, tasty primate called a bush baby might be sleeping. What a rude way to be woken up!

A chimpazee pokes around looking for yummy termites.

CHAPTER FOUR

BUILDERS
AND SHAPERS

A tent-making bat in its leafy haven.

Animals have found ways to make clever use of stuff like sticks, leaves, and stones for housing as well as for catching food. The tent-making bat lives throughout parts of tropical America. When it is ready to roost for the day, the bat chews the center part of a big leaf. By making the center of the leaf weak, the sides droop down, forming a kind of tent. Several bats can climb inside and hang upside-down from the leaf's rib, protected from the rain, wind, and predators.

22

Weaver ants weaving a home.

Weaver ants also like to live in leafy tents in sub-Saharan Africa. They create giant colonies of leaf nests in the treetops. One colony of ants can spread through many trees and include several queen ants. The ants build their nests by weaving several leaves together using silk that is produced by their larvae.

Fast Fact

Weaver ants like to eat the pests that eat fruit, so fruit-tree growers encourage the ants to live on their plantations. The growers even build bamboo bridges between the fruit trees so the ants can move around more easily.

A HOUSE OF WOOD

Trees provide housing for lots of other animals besides bats and ants. Many kinds of birds build nests in branches. Other birds drill nests in the trunks of trees. Hornbills do more than just make use of a nice tree hole for a home. Once a pair of hornbills finds the perfect tree hollow for a nest, they line it with grass and leaves. Then, the female seals herself inside the hollow using vomit, poop, and mud that the male brings to her. She leaves just a tiny slit so that he can drop food in for her and her chicks. Once the chicks are about half grown, she breaks out to freedom. The chicks reseal themselves inside the hollow until they are ready to fly.

A hornbill checking on his family inside the tree.

Many kinds of hornets, yellow jackets, and wasps have another nesting use for trees. A queen picks

24

a safe place such as a human shelter, under a branch, or in an abandoned animal burrow. She makes wood pulp by chewing up bits of wood from trees. She carefully spits out the pulp to build her nest. The outside of the nest dries into strong paper. Inside, the queen creates paper cells, laying an egg in each one as she goes. Babies are born and grow up to be workers that continue building and tending the nest.

A paper house built with wood and spit.

A HOUSE OF MUD OR POOP

The mud dauber wasp prefers mud for building its nurseries. The female collects mud and carries it to her nursery site. She creates cells by spreading the mud carefully into a tube shape. After she lays an egg in a cell, she captures a few insects or spiders

A mud dauber wasp seems to sing while she works.

and crams them inside with the egg. Then she seals it all up with mud and continues on to the next cell. Later, the eggs hatch, and the wasp larvae have dinner waiting in their mud nurseries.

Birds such as swallows also know a thing or two about mud nesting. Their ancestors were burrowers. Many kinds of swallows build nests out of mud that they gather from puddles, ponds, and stream banks. Cliff swallows like to nest in groups. A pair builds a gourd-shaped mud nest in a community with other cliff swallows.

Cliff swallows like to live in close communities.

The swallows often help each other and even build nests that branch off other nests. Colonies of cliff swallows can be found on cliffs and buildings, as well as under bridges. In some colonies the nests can number in the thousands.

Even poop comes in handy as a homemade nest of sorts. Dung beetles use other animals' poop as a place to raise their young. A pair will form a ball out of a bit of poop and work together to roll it away and bury it inside a tunnel. The female lays an egg in the ball and then seals up the tunnel. The beetles will do this for each egg the female lays. Their little grubs will have something good to munch on after they hatch. Dung beetles live on every continent except Antarctica.

Male and female dung beetles work together on their poop paradise.

CHAPTER FIVE

UNDERWATER AND UNDERGROUND

The world beneath the water's surface is full of potential building materials and opportunities for safe housing, including living creatures! The pearl fish is an eel-like fish that has found the perfect place to live underwater. It seeks out a friendly creature called a sea cucumber, which happens to breathe through its anus. When the sea cucumber takes a breath, the pearlfish swims inside its anus. The pearlfish hangs out inside the body cavity, where it's safe. It swims out at night to feed and

This male shell-brooding cichlid attracts a female with his shell collection.

28

shoots back inside in the morning. Home sweet home!

For protection, the hermit crab takes over an empty shell originally made by another animal. As it grows, it crawls out of one shell and moves into another, bigger one. A fish called a shell-brooding cichlid uses shells, too. A male searches for empty shells and carries them one by one to his nesting site. His shell collection attracts females to his lair. A female chooses a shell in which to lay her eggs. The nursery shell protects her eggs from predators. A successful cichlid has lots of pretty shells.

The smartest undersea shell user seems to be the veined octopus. This eight-legged mollusk lives in the tropics. It digs up coconut shell halves that have fallen into the ocean. Then it tiptoes around

The Leach's hermit crab will let a cloak anemone, which has stinging tentacles, attach to its shell. The anemone stings anything that tries to attack the crab and enjoys the scraps of food the hermit crab drops in return.

This veined octopus walks around carrying its coconut shell house with it.

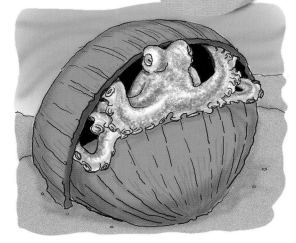

with the halves suctioned under its body. When the octopus senses danger or just decides to stop and rest, it pulls out the shells and climbs inside, pulling the halves closed over its body. This discovery by a team of researchers qualified the veined octopus as another tool-using animal. It is the first tool user without a backbone!

LIVING IN A BUBBLE

A diving bell spider snatches a fishy snack from its bubble lair.

The diving bell spider of north and central Europe is the only spider that spends its entire life underwater. This spider weaves a diving bell, which it fills up with air from bubbles on the water's surface. The air-filled bell lets oxygen in and carbon dioxide out, so the spider can stay inside for a long time without adding more oxygen. Silk threads hold the diving bell in place among pond weeds. When something yummy bounces on a thread, the spider darts out and snags it.

EARTH HAVENS

Many land-dwelling animals find safe havens underground, where they are protected from extreme weather and predators. Even birds have figured out that an underground tunnel is a good place to raise a family. The kingfisher is a bird that lives throughout the tropics and temperate regions of the world. It makes a nest in burrows it digs with its feet. The kingfisher likes to dig on a creek bank, making a tunnel 3 to 6 feet (1 to 2 m) long. At the end of the tunnel is a nesting chamber where its eggs are laid and chicks are raised. The Carmen bee-eater is another kind of bird that likes to dig a tunnel for nesting. It lives in watery

Beautiful Carmen bee-eaters dig nesting tunnels on a riverbank.

31

Fast Fact

There can be more than a million earthworms tunneling around on 1 acre (0.4 hectare) of land.

places in parts of Africa. When a beeeater finds a good nesting spot on a riverbank, it will fly and slam its beak against the spot until it has a good-size hole started. Then it will cling to the entrance and keep digging with its feet and beak until the tunnel chamber is just right.

Other animals live underground practically full-time. Using special body parts and skills, these animals spend most of their lives tunneling and burrowing.

You might see earthworms hanging out in a puddle during the day. But earthworms spend most of their time underground, consuming matter in the soil and pooping out **castings** as they burrow along. Their tunneling and pooping mixes up the soil, adds nutrients to it, and helps get air to plant roots.

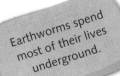

Earthworms spend most of their lives underground.

UNDERGROUND CITIES

The naked mole rats of Africa live in colonies with a single

queen, sort of like bees do. There can be as few as twenty and as many as three hundred naked mole rats living and working in one huge underground city. Their home has a nursery chamber for the queen and her babies, feeding chambers, and even a bathroom. Mole rats work together to make a tunnel. They line up nose to tail. The mole rat in front breaks through the soil with its teeth. The next in line uses its feet and toe hairs to sweep the dirt backward. The last mole rat in the line kicks up the dirt onto the surface outside the tunnel, making a volcano-shaped hill.

These two naked mole rats need to decide who gets to back out!

Prairie dogs also live in huge, underground communities called prairie dog towns. They do not have a single queen like naked mole rats do. There are lots of nurseries, sleeping chambers, and toilet rooms in their towns. Other animals might live in the burrows with them, such as snakes and burrowing owls.

Fast Fact

One Texas prairie dog town covered about 25,000 square miles (65,000 square kilometers) and housed an estimated 400 million prairie dogs.

CHAPTER SIX

AMAZING STRUCTURES

Just about all animals have a special place they call home. Some homes are as modest as a cococnut shell for a single octopus, while others are as elaborate as an extensive underground town that houses millions of prairie dogs.

In Africa you might see a 9,000-pound (4,100-kg) elephant scratching its behind on a tall structure that isn't a rock or a tree stump. This itching post is a towering termite mound build by African mound-building termites. Millions

A termite mound's tower vents help to control the temperature inside.

of termites live and work in one of these mounds, made from mud and termite spit. Some termite mounds are more than 20 feet (6 m) high. What goes on inside? Termite mounds contain an elaborate tunnel system that includes hundreds of chambers above and below ground level. The mounds have places to nurture eggs and store food as well as a special royal chamber for the queen. They even have a chamber for garbage. There are also special chambers where the termites grow fungus, which they eat and feed to their young. The fungus needs to be just the right temperature to grow. The termites tunnel out ventilation passageways that come out of the top and sides of the mound. They adjust the indoor temperature by controlling the air currents coming in and going out of the mound. They do this by digging new vents and closing others.

Termite Architecture

The Eastgate Centre in Harare, Zimbabwe, was designed to mimic the way termites make use of ventilation shafts in their mounds. The building's temperature is regulated using a series of heating and cooling vents, much like those used in termite mounds.

AMAZING BIRD NESTS

A little wading bird from Kenya called the hammerhead stork constructs a strong nest, too. Using sticks, a pair of hammerhead storks builds a platform and sturdy walls in the fork of a tree. Once the birds have made a big bowl shape, they add a thick roof using sticks and mud. They leave a small entrance, creating what looks like a house of sticks. They might decorate the roof with things like snakeskin, bones, and trinkets they find. A single nest can be more than 6 feet (2 m) high and wide, with a roof strong enough for an adult human to stand on. One pair often builds several giant structures before it decides on one. Other animals, such as owls, ducks, snakes, and lizards, appreciate the free housing.

A hammerhead stork nest can be strong enough for a human to stand on.

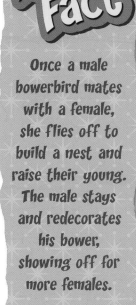

A satin bowerbird loves using blue trinkets to decorate his house.

The male bowerbird can out-decorate the hammerhead stork. This bird, from Australia and New Guinea, creates an elaborate structure called a bower to attract a mate. Each has its own design. The structure might be a wide arch made of sticks, moss, and leaves. The bowerbird may set up a tall, decorated pole. Once the foundation is built, the bird decorates the bower with whatever cool trinkets he can find. He will use things like berries, flowers, feathers, and fruit. Some bowerbirds seem especially fond of human-made objects, such as coins and silverware. The satin bowerbird is famous for collecting mostly blue items. He might even paint the walls of his structure with chewed-up blueberries.

The sociable weavers of South Africa and southern Namibia are probably the most amazing of all the nesters. These birds weave one huge tree nest

Fast Fact

Once a male bowerbird mates with a female, she flies off to build a nest and raise their young. The male stays and redecorates his bower, showing off for more females.

37

A sociable weaver nest colony can house hundreds of birds and other animals.

for an entire colony. The giant apartment building-like structures have entrances underneath and dozens of nesting chambers inside that are similar to the chambers in a prairie dog town. The cozy apartments are lined with soft materials like fur, fluff, and cotton. One nest can house hundreds of birds. Other animals might take advantage of any extra chambers, and some birds nest on top of the structure. The well-insulated nest stays warm on cold nights and cool on hot days. Throughout the year the birds work together to maintain the gigantic structure.

LIVING SHELTERS

There is an even bigger communal house that animals create by making use of their bodies. A coral reef is a collection of animals that live on the dead remains of their ancestors. Corals are

collections of hundreds or even thousands of tiny animals called coral **polyps**. A polyp lives inside a shell made of a hard material. Coral polyps join together to form different shapes, like fingers, branches, boulders, and mushrooms. Coral reefs start to form when the creatures attach themselves to rocks or other hard surfaces in shallow water. Most coral polyps don't move once they fasten themselves. They catch food that floats by using tentacles and stingers. When a polyp dies, its shell becomes part of the coral reef. The reef grows and grows for thousands of years. Thousands of other sea-dwelling creatures find havens in a coral reef.

Fast Fact

The largest coral reef on Earth is the Great Barrier Reef, off the coast of Queensland, Australia. It is more than 1,200 miles (1,900 kilometers) long.

39

CHAPTER SEVEN

BUSY BUSY BUSY

One animal constructs what is probably the most amazing engineering marvel in the animal kingdom. A beaver leaves home at about two years old. It travels streams and rivers, seeking a partner and a good place to live. When two beavers meet up, they set right to work on their new home.

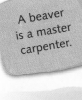

A beaver is a master carpenter.

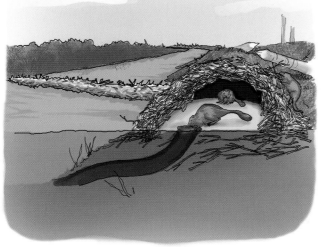

The first step is staking a claim to the site they choose. A beaver piles up mounds of mud and muck close to the water. Then it spreads a bit of beaver stink, called castor, on the mound. This is a message

40

to other beavers to back off. If a castor mound is close to another beaver's territory, that beaver might pack on more mud and spread its own special stink on the mound. So there! Some castor mounds grow to be huge if several beavers are arguing over territory.

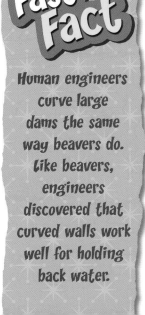

A beaver can make quick work of logging the area.

The next step is to gather brush and place it on just the right spot in the stream or river. Beavers gnaw down branches and trees along the banks. They carefully float the construction materials to the dam site, using their teeth to guide them. They lay down the branches with the bases pointing downstream. If the water has a strong current, they might curve the structures of the jutting part faces upstream.

Next, the beavers add rocks and mud to seal and strengthen the dam as they continue to build.

Fast Fact

Human engineers curve large dams the same way beavers do. Like beavers, engineers discovered that curved walls work well for holding back water.

Amazing Dams

Some beaver dams are huge and very old. The longest one recorded so far is about 2,800 feet (850 m) long. Researchers believe that more than one beaver colony built it.

They continue to add sticks, rocks, trash, and whatever else they might run across to build up the dam. The resulting material is the beaver version of concrete. Where concrete is made from sand, rocks, and cement mixed with water, beavers create a mix of sticks, rocks, debris, and mud for their dams.

Beavers make their dams wider and taller as the water rises. Their goal is to create a pond deep enough not to freeze solid during the winter. They store food in the water under the surface ice.

SAFE HAVEN FOR MANY

By damming a stream and creating a pond and surrounding wetlands, beavers create a safe haven in which to raise a family.

While beavers build a dam, they take **refuge** along the stream banks and rest during the day. When the dam is holding water to their satisfaction, it's time to build a lodge. The lodge is also made with sticks and mud, but it is not as carefully laid out as the dam. The beavers just heap up a big pile of sticks and mud. The heap's base is under-water and extends above the surface. Some lodges are 12 to 15 feet (3.5 to 4.5 m) above the water's surface.

After they have a nice big heap of sticks and mud, beavers swim underwater and gnaw a tunnel up through the new lodge. When they are above water, they scoop out a living room. If any animal tries to break in to the lodge, such as a bear, cougar, or a wolf, the beavers can escape by swimming down through the underwater entrance and away from the lodge. The structure is usually too strong for predators to get through, anyway.

A beaver pond is a haven for beavers and many other animals.

FOOD WATERWAYS

Beavers are terrific swimmers, but they do not move very fast on land. Dragging heavy branches

Fast Fact

Beavers can stay underwater for fifteen minutes or more before they need to come up for air. They can swim a great distance in that amount of time!

slows them down even more. So these amazing engineers developed yet another trick. They dig out canals in the water that lead to good places to gather food. The canals spread out from the main ponds, sometimes over 700 feet (210 m) into the woods. Then the beavers can swim to the food and float their bounty back home. Beavers stay busy throughout the spring, summer, and fall. Winter is a time for hanging out with the family, eating, and taking naps in their cozy lodge.

Many members of the animal world have figured out amazing ways to construct a safe haven, snag a meal, and make use of protected food storage. Many animals have come up with extraordinary ways to use whatever is at hand as tools and building materials. Their clever methods help them to survive. In recent years we have learned that some animals appear to be a lot smarter than we thought!

A beaver brings a tasty branch to store for winter.

GLOSSARY

adaptation the act of adjusting to improve a relationship with the environment

ancestor an early plant or animal from which others evolved

camouflage to blend in with surroundings

castings masses of earth ejected by a burrowing worm

cell a chamber

excretions waste materials that are discharged from the body

larva an immature form of an animal

mandible a jaw or jawbone

polyp a creature with a cylindrical body and mouth opening that is usually surrounded by tentacles

refuge a place of safety

rostrum a stiff snout, similar to a beak, on the head of an animal

secretions substances that are made from cells or bodily fluids

FIND OUT MORE

BOOKS

Linden, Eugene. *The Octopus and the Orangutan.* New York, New York: Dutton, 2003.

Pryor, Kimberley Jane. *Tricky Behavior.* New York: Marshall Cavendish Benchmark, 2009.

Uhlenbroek, Charlotte. *Animal Life.* New York, New York: DK Publishing, 2008.

WEBSITES

Animal Diversity Web
http://animaldiversity.ummz.umich.edu/site/index.html

Animal Planet
http://animal.discovery.com/

Discovery Kids
http://kids.discovery.com/

National Geographic Kids
http://kids.nationalgeographic.com/

INDEX

All photographs and illustrations are in **boldface**.

ABOUT THE AUTHOR

ROBIN KOONTZ grew up in a wild suburb of Maryland and later lived in West Virginia. She learned from some great people how to respect every living creature. Robin now lives with her husband and various critters in the Coast Range mountains of western Oregon. She shares her office space with spiders and whatever they happen to catch.